PRINCEWILL LAGANG

The Retail Maestro: Amancio Ortega's Journey to Zara Dominance

First published by PRINCEWILL LAGANG 2023

Copyright © 2023 by Princewill Lagang

All rights reserved. No part of this publication may be reproduced, stored or transmitted in any form or by any means, electronic, mechanical, photocopying, recording, scanning, or otherwise without written permission from the publisher. It is illegal to copy this book, post it to a website, or distribute it by any other means without permission.

Princewill Lagang asserts the moral right to be identified as the author of this work.

First edition

This book was professionally typeset on Reedsy.
Find out more at reedsy.com

Contents

1	Introduction	1
2	The Early Threads	3
3	The Tapestry Unraveled	5
4	The Threads of Transformation	7
5	Global Influence: Zara's Impact on Fashion and...	9
6	Resilience in the Face of Change: Zara's Evolution in a...	11
7	Legacy Woven: Amancio Ortega's Enduring Impact and Zara's...	13
8	Threads of Inspiration: Zara's Influence on the Fashion...	15
9	Beyond Fashion: Zara's Cultural and Economic Impact	17
10	The Next Chapter: Zara's Ongoing Evolution and Future...	19
11	Threads of Reflection: Zara's Enduring Legacy and Lessons...	21
12	The Unwritten Chapter: Exploring Possibilities and Beyond	23
13	Threads of Gratitude: Celebrating Zara's Enduring Impact	25
14	Summary	27

1

Introduction

In the ever-evolving tapestry of the fashion industry, certain threads stand out, weaving stories of innovation, resilience, and influence. "Zara: Threads of Innovation and Legacy" invites you on a captivating journey through the history, impact, and future horizons of one of the fashion world's most iconic brands. From its modest beginnings in a small town to its global prominence, Zara has not only transformed the way we experience fashion but has left an indelible mark on the cultural and economic fabric of our interconnected world.

Founded by the visionary Amancio Ortega, Zara's story is one of pioneering "fast fashion," a model that revolutionized how we consume and perceive style. This narrative unfolds across chapters, each revealing a different facet of Zara's evolution. From its technological embrace to a commitment to sustainability, the brand's influence extends beyond the runway to touch the lives of consumers, artisans, and communities worldwide.

As we traverse through Zara's legacy, we delve into the intricacies of its global impact, exploring how it has shaped trends, fostered sustainability, and contributed to cultural conversations. The narrative not only reflects on the brand's past but also peeks into the future, contemplating the uncharted threads that may weave into the next chapters of Zara's extraordinary story.

Join us on this exploration of "Zara: Threads of Innovation and Legacy," where each page unfolds a tapestry of inspiration, reflecting the resilience of a brand that continues to shape the very fabric of the fashion industry.

2

The Early Threads

Title: "The Retail Maestro: Amancio Ortega's Journey to Zara Dominance"

In the bustling town of Busdongo de Arbás, nestled in the picturesque landscape of northern Spain, a visionary was born on March 28, 1936. Amancio Ortega, the future retail magnate and founder of Zara, came into the world in a modest family, where his father worked as a railway worker. Little did anyone know that this unassuming beginning would lay the foundation for one of the most influential figures in the fashion industry.

Amancio's early years were marked by a quiet determination and a keen eye for opportunity. The post-World War II era was a time of rebuilding and economic resurgence, and young Ortega found himself drawn to the world of entrepreneurship. His first foray into business began at the age of 14 when he took up a job as a delivery boy for a local shirt maker. This seemingly inconspicuous role would become the starting point for a lifelong passion for textiles and fashion.

As a young man, Ortega honed his skills working for various local clothing stores. His ability to understand customer preferences and anticipate trends quickly set him apart. It was during this time that he developed a deep appreciation for the art of retail, realizing that success hinged not only on offering quality products but also on understanding and responding to the ever-evolving demands of the consumer.

In the early 1960s, fueled by a burning ambition and an unwavering belief in his instincts, Ortega took the leap into entrepreneurship. Alongside his wife, Rosalía Mera, he founded Confecciones Goa, a small dressing gown and housecoat manufacturing company. The venture gained traction, and Ortega's knack for understanding the market allowed the couple to expand their product line.

The turning point in Ortega's career came in 1975 when he opened the first store under the brand name Zara in La Coruña, Spain. This marked the birth of a retail revolution, as Zara's unique approach to fashion retailing disrupted the traditional industry model. Ortega pioneered the concept of "fast fashion" – a strategy that involved quickly responding to emerging trends and efficiently delivering affordable, stylish clothing to consumers.

This chapter delves into the early life and formative years of Amancio Ortega, shedding light on the experiences and insights that shaped his entrepreneurial spirit. As we follow his journey from a small town in Spain to the inception of Zara, we uncover the seeds of innovation and determination that would later propel him to the summit of the global fashion industry.

3

The Tapestry Unraveled

Title: "Innovations and Challenges: Zara's Rise in the Fast Fashion Tapestry"

As Amancio Ortega's Zara embarked on its journey, the fashion landscape was undergoing a seismic shift. Chapter 2 explores the key innovations and challenges that defined Zara's ascent in the fast-paced world of fashion retail.

Zara's success wasn't just about selling clothes; it was a testament to Ortega's ability to revolutionize the industry. The chapter delves into the groundbreaking "fast fashion" model that Zara pioneered, emphasizing the importance of speed and agility in responding to consumer trends. The company's vertically integrated supply chain, from design to manufacturing and distribution, allowed it to bring new styles to market at unprecedented speeds.

In the early years, Zara's success was buoyed by its unique approach to inventory management. Ortega's team, led by a cadre of skilled designers and trend forecasters, ensured that the stores consistently carried the latest styles.

The "see now, buy now" philosophy resonated with consumers, creating a sense of urgency and exclusivity that set Zara apart from its competitors.

However, as Zara's star rose, challenges emerged. The rapid expansion and demand for quick turnarounds in fashion trends placed immense pressure on the supply chain. The chapter explores how Ortega and his team navigated these challenges, innovating and fine-tuning their processes to maintain the delicate balance between speed and quality.

Another aspect of Zara's success was its meticulous attention to customer feedback. Ortega, known for his humility and willingness to adapt, placed a premium on understanding and meeting customer expectations. The chapter unfolds the story of Zara's customer-centric approach, illustrating how it cultivated a loyal customer base that eagerly anticipated each new collection.

Internationally, Zara expanded its footprint, setting the stage for its global dominance. The narrative explores how the brand strategically entered new markets, adapting its offerings to suit diverse consumer tastes. The company's ability to balance a global presence with local relevance became a hallmark of its success.

As Zara wove its way through the intricacies of the fashion industry, this chapter unveils the threads of innovation, resilience, and adaptability that formed the fabric of its success. It sets the stage for the continued evolution of Zara and its indelible impact on the fashion retail landscape.

4

The Threads of Transformation

Title: "Tech and Trends: Zara's Digital Metamorphosis"

In the ever-evolving landscape of fashion retail, the digital age posed both a challenge and an opportunity. Chapter 3 explores how Zara, under the visionary leadership of Amancio Ortega, navigated the digital transformation that reshaped consumer behaviors and expectations.

As the 21st century dawned, Zara recognized the significance of technology in shaping the future of retail. This chapter unravels the strategic investments and innovations that propelled Zara into the digital realm. From the integration of advanced data analytics to the implementation of state-of-the-art inventory management systems, Zara's technological embrace aimed to enhance both efficiency and customer experience.

One pivotal aspect of Zara's digital strategy was its foray into e-commerce. The chapter delves into how the brand seamlessly translated its in-store experience into the online space, allowing customers to engage with Zara's fast fashion from the comfort of their homes. The digital storefront became an extension of Zara's commitment to immediacy and accessibility, enabling the brand to connect with a global audience.

The rise of social media and the emergence of influencers presented a new frontier for fashion marketing. Zara, known for its discretion in traditional advertising, embraced this shift with agility. The chapter explores how the brand leveraged social media platforms to engage with its audience, using influencers to showcase its latest collections and create buzz around new releases.

Yet, with technological advancements came the challenge of maintaining a delicate balance between tradition and innovation. Zara's commitment to maintaining the essence of its brand identity while embracing digital trends is a central theme in this chapter. The story unfolds as Zara modernizes its approach without losing the essence of what made it a retail powerhouse.

The narrative also touches upon challenges faced by Zara in the digital era, such as cybersecurity concerns and the need to constantly evolve to meet the ever-changing demands of tech-savvy consumers.

Chapter 3 paints a vivid picture of Zara's digital metamorphosis, illustrating how the brand seamlessly integrated technology into its DNA to stay at the forefront of the fast fashion revolution. As the threads of tradition intertwined with the fabric of innovation, Zara continued to evolve, ensuring its enduring relevance in the dynamic world of fashion retail.

5

Global Influence: Zara's Impact on Fashion and Sustainability

Title: "Sustainable Threads and Global Trends: Zara's Influence Unraveled"

As Zara continued to weave its way through the global fashion landscape, Chapter 4 explores the brand's impact on industry trends and its efforts to address the growing importance of sustainability.

The chapter begins by examining Zara's influence on fashion trends worldwide. From the runways of Paris to the streets of Tokyo, Zara's fast fashion model not only shaped consumer expectations but also influenced the broader industry. The narrative unfolds how the brand's ability to swiftly translate runway trends into affordable, accessible clothing democratized fashion, making high-end styles accessible to a broader audience.

However, with this global influence came heightened scrutiny regarding sustainability and ethical practices within the fashion industry. Zara, under the leadership of Amancio Ortega, recognized the imperative to address environmental concerns and social responsibility. The chapter delves into Zara's journey towards sustainability, exploring initiatives such as the use of eco-friendly materials, ethical sourcing practices, and the implementation of recycling programs.

Amid the fashion industry's increasing focus on sustainability, Zara's commitment to the environment becomes a focal point of the narrative. The chapter unravels the brand's efforts to balance its commitment to delivering on-trend, affordable fashion with a growing responsibility towards minimizing its ecological footprint.

The story also explores Zara's engagement with social and cultural issues. From supporting diverse and inclusive campaigns to championing local artisans and traditional craftsmanship, Zara's influence extended beyond fashion trends, making an impact on the broader societal conversation.

Furthermore, the chapter sheds light on Zara's collaborations with renowned designers and artists, showcasing how these partnerships contributed not only to the brand's cachet but also to the evolving narrative of the fashion industry.

As the global fashion tapestry continued to transform, Zara's role in shaping trends, fostering sustainability, and influencing societal conversations became increasingly prominent. Chapter 4 captures the threads of Zara's global impact, weaving together its influence on fashion, sustainability, and social responsibility into a rich narrative that reflects the brand's multifaceted legacy.

6

Resilience in the Face of Change: Zara's Evolution in a Dynamic World

Title: "Adapting Threads: Zara's Resilience in a Shifting Landscape"

In the ever-evolving world of fashion, resilience is a cornerstone of success. Chapter 5 delves into Zara's ability to navigate through challenges, adapt to changing consumer behaviors, and maintain its position as a global fashion powerhouse.

The chapter begins by exploring the impact of geopolitical and economic shifts on Zara's operations. From economic recessions to geopolitical tensions, Zara faced a myriad of challenges that tested the brand's resilience. The narrative unravels how Amancio Ortega's leadership and Zara's agile business model allowed the brand to weather storms, adapting its strategies to overcome external pressures.

Consumer preferences and shopping habits underwent significant transformations in the digital age. With the rise of e-commerce giants and changes in consumer expectations, brick-and-mortar retailers faced a new reality.

Chapter 5 examines Zara's response to the digital disruption, exploring how the brand evolved its online presence, embraced omnichannel strategies, and maintained a harmonious balance between physical stores and the digital realm.

The story also delves into Zara's approach to inclusivity and diversity, reflecting the brand's commitment to resonating with a global audience. Initiatives such as diverse casting in campaigns and inclusivity in sizing underscored Zara's dedication to catering to the diverse tastes and preferences of its customer base.

In an era marked by increased consciousness about ethical business practices, Zara's stance on corporate social responsibility takes center stage. The chapter unfolds the brand's initiatives to improve labor conditions, reduce environmental impact, and contribute to social causes, showcasing Zara's commitment to being a responsible global citizen.

As Zara continued to evolve, the narrative explores the brand's exploration of new markets and expansion into emerging economies. The challenges and triumphs faced in establishing a foothold in regions with distinct cultural nuances add depth to the story of Zara's global journey.

Chapter 5 weaves together the threads of resilience, adaptability, and corporate responsibility, illustrating how Zara not only survived but thrived in a dynamic and competitive landscape. The narrative sets the stage for Zara's continued evolution, emphasizing the brand's enduring ability to navigate change and emerge stronger in the face of adversity.

7

Legacy Woven: Amancio Ortega's Enduring Impact and Zara's Future Threads

Title: "A Tapestry of Influence: Amancio Ortega's Legacy and Zara's Uncharted Horizons"

As Zara's journey unfolded, Chapter 6 takes a reflective turn, examining the enduring legacy of its visionary founder, Amancio Ortega, and casting a gaze toward the future, exploring the brand's uncharted horizons.

The chapter begins by delving into the leadership philosophy of Amancio Ortega. As the driving force behind Zara, Ortega's hands-on approach, commitment to innovation, and emphasis on empowering the creative minds within the company have left an indelible mark on the brand's DNA. The narrative weaves together anecdotes of Ortega's leadership style, illustrating how his entrepreneurial spirit and dedication to excellence became the guiding principles for Zara's success.

In exploring Ortega's legacy, the chapter examines his philanthropic endeavors and contributions to societal causes. From investments in healthcare to support for education, Ortega's impact extended beyond the realm of fashion, portraying a leader who understood the broader responsibilities that come with influence and success.

As Zara looks to the future, the narrative shifts to the brand's ongoing commitment to innovation. The chapter unravels how Zara continues to leverage technology, data analytics, and sustainability initiatives to stay at the forefront of the fashion industry. The brand's exploration of emerging technologies, such as artificial intelligence and augmented reality, adds a futuristic dimension to the narrative.

In the context of a rapidly changing retail landscape, the chapter explores Zara's strategies for staying relevant in the digital age. The brand's engagement with social media, e-commerce, and evolving consumer behaviors showcases its adaptability and foresight.

The story concludes by peering into Zara's uncharted horizons. Whether venturing into new markets, experimenting with novel business models, or embracing the next wave of fashion trends, the narrative hints at the brand's readiness to continue shaping the future of fashion.

Chapter 6, with a reflective tone, encapsulates the threads of Zara's journey, paying tribute to the legacy of Amancio Ortega while signaling the brand's readiness to navigate unexplored territories. The story of Zara, woven with innovation, resilience, and a commitment to excellence, sets the stage for the brand's continued influence on the global fashion tapestry.

8

Threads of Inspiration: Zara's Influence on the Fashion Ecosystem

Title: "Fashion Ecosystem Unveiled: Zara's Enduring Impact and Inspirations"

In the vast tapestry of the fashion ecosystem, Zara stands as a beacon of influence and inspiration. Chapter 7 unravels the threads of Zara's impact on the broader fashion landscape, exploring how the brand has shaped trends, inspired competitors, and contributed to the evolution of the industry.

The chapter begins by delving into Zara's role as a trendsetter. From runway to street fashion, Zara's ability to swiftly interpret and deliver the latest trends to the mass market has set a precedent for the industry. The narrative unfolds the brand's impact on the democratization of fashion, making high-end styles accessible to a diverse global audience.

Zara's influence on the fast fashion model is dissected, examining how competitors and newcomers to the industry have sought to replicate the brand's successful formula. The chapter explores the phenomenon of "Zaraization" in the fashion world, where speed, efficiency, and a customer-centric approach have become benchmarks for success.

As a testament to Zara's global resonance, the narrative explores the brand's collaborations with international designers and artists. The chapter unveils how these partnerships not only elevated Zara's prestige but also contributed to a cross-pollination of ideas within the fashion ecosystem.

The story then shifts to the sustainable fashion movement, where Zara's journey towards eco-friendly practices serves as a source of inspiration for the industry. The chapter examines how Zara's initiatives to reduce environmental impact and promote ethical practices have influenced other brands to embrace sustainability as a core value.

Zara's retail strategies, both online and offline, are dissected to uncover their impact on the evolving consumer journey. The narrative explores how Zara's omnichannel approach, from in-store experiences to e-commerce, has become a benchmark for retailers seeking to navigate the digital age successfully.

The chapter concludes by examining Zara's place in the future fashion landscape. As the industry continues to evolve, the narrative hints at Zara's potential to continue shaping trends, fostering sustainability, and serving as a touchstone for innovation.

Chapter 7, filled with stories of inspiration and influence, paints a picture of Zara's role within the broader fashion ecosystem. The brand's impact on trends, retail strategies, and sustainability serves as a testament to its enduring legacy and its ongoing contribution to the dynamic world of fashion.

9

Beyond Fashion: Zara's Cultural and Economic Impact

Title: "Cultural Weaving: Zara's Global Influence and Economic Legacy"

As Zara's threads became woven into the fabric of global fashion, Chapter 8 explores the brand's profound cultural impact and economic legacy, transcending the realm of apparel to touch various facets of society.

The chapter begins by unraveling Zara's cultural influence, delving into its role as a cultural touchstone and symbol of contemporary style. From its fashion-forward designs to its innovative marketing campaigns, Zara has become synonymous with modernity and trendiness. The narrative explores how the brand's presence in popular culture, from films to social media, has contributed to shaping perceptions of fashion on a global scale.

Zara's impact on local economies and the broader fashion industry is examined in-depth. The brand's emphasis on local production, coupled with its global reach, has created a ripple effect in communities around the world. The chapter delves into the economic ecosystems Zara has fostered, from supporting local artisans to influencing entire fashion districts.

The narrative then turns to the brand's engagement with diverse cultural elements. Zara's incorporation of traditional craftsmanship, collaborations with artists from various backgrounds, and celebration of global diversity are dissected to uncover how the brand has become a cultural ambassador in the world of fashion.

As Zara navigates the complexities of international markets, the chapter explores the brand's diplomatic role. Zara's presence in diverse regions and its adaptation to local tastes are examined as the brand's way of fostering cultural understanding through the universal language of fashion.

Economically, Zara's success story is not just confined to the fashion industry. The chapter delves into the brand's contribution to employment, entrepreneurship, and economic development. Zara's ability to adapt to changing economic landscapes, from economic downturns to periods of growth, showcases its resilience and its role as an economic force.

The chapter concludes by examining Zara's legacy in the broader context of global culture and economy. As the brand continues to weave its influence across borders, the narrative hints at the lasting impact of Zara on the cultural and economic tapestry of our interconnected world.

Chapter 8 unfolds the rich layers of Zara's cultural influence and economic legacy, showcasing how the brand's threads have become interwoven with the very fabric of society, transcending the boundaries of fashion to leave an indelible mark on the global stage.

10

The Next Chapter: Zara's Ongoing Evolution and Future Horizons

Title: "Uncharted Threads: Zara's Ongoing Journey and Future Frontiers"

As Zara stands at the crossroads of its storied history, Chapter 9 takes a forward-looking perspective, exploring the brand's ongoing evolution and venturing into the uncharted threads that will shape its future.

The chapter begins by examining Zara's response to the dynamic forces of change. From technological innovations to shifts in consumer behavior, the narrative unravels how Zara continues to adapt, embracing emerging trends and redefining its strategies to maintain its position as a trailblazer in the fashion industry.

Zara's commitment to sustainability is brought into sharper focus, as the chapter explores how the brand's eco-friendly initiatives have evolved. The narrative delves into Zara's efforts to further reduce its environmental footprint, incorporate circular economy principles, and champion ethical practices in the fashion ecosystem.

The exploration of Zara's global footprint extends into new markets and innovative business models. The chapter unfolds how the brand strategically expands its presence, whether through collaborations, partnerships, or the exploration of untapped regions. The narrative hints at Zara's potential to continue influencing the global fashion landscape while staying attuned to local nuances.

The integration of technology in retail is a central theme in this chapter. The narrative examines how Zara harnesses the power of artificial intelligence, data analytics, and immersive technologies to enhance the customer experience, both online and in physical stores. The unfolding story suggests that Zara's commitment to tech-driven solutions will be a pivotal aspect of its future growth.

The chapter also explores Zara's role in shaping industry standards. Whether through responsible business practices, inclusivity initiatives, or innovative design approaches, the narrative suggests that Zara's influence will extend beyond its own brand, setting benchmarks for the broader fashion ecosystem.

The story concludes with a glimpse into Zara's future horizons. The uncharted threads represent not just challenges but also opportunities for growth, innovation, and cultural impact. As Zara continues its journey into the next chapter, the narrative leaves room for anticipation and excitement, inviting readers to witness the unfolding of a new era in the brand's remarkable history.

Chapter 9 paints a portrait of Zara on the cusp of a new era, capturing the brand's ongoing evolution, commitment to innovation, and anticipation of the uncharted threads that will shape its future.

11

Threads of Reflection: Zara's Enduring Legacy and Lessons for the Future

Title: "Legacy Woven, Lessons Unveiled: Zara's Impact and Insights"

In the final chapter of this narrative journey through Zara's remarkable story, Chapter 10 serves as a tapestry of reflection, unraveling the brand's enduring legacy and extracting valuable lessons for the future of the fashion industry.

The chapter begins by revisiting key moments in Zara's journey, from its humble origins to its status as a global fashion icon. The narrative reflects on the transformative impact of Zara on the industry, underscoring how the brand's innovative approach to fast fashion, commitment to sustainability, and adaptability to change have set a benchmark for success.

As the story unfolds, the chapter explores the cultural, economic, and technological shifts that have shaped Zara's trajectory. It reflects on how the brand navigated challenges, capitalized on opportunities, and remained resilient in the face of a rapidly evolving fashion landscape.

Zara's influence on consumer behavior is examined in-depth, revealing insights into the psychology of fast fashion and the brand's ability to create a sense of urgency and exclusivity. The chapter delves into how Zara's customer-centric approach and responsiveness to trends have influenced expectations within the fashion industry.

The narrative then shifts to the broader implications of Zara's success, exploring how the brand has paved the way for a more sustainable and inclusive fashion ecosystem. The chapter reflects on Zara's contributions to ethical practices, diversity, and the global conversation surrounding responsible business in the 21st century.

An important theme in this chapter is the leadership legacy of Amancio Ortega. The narrative reflects on Ortega's visionary leadership style, humility, and hands-on approach, extracting valuable leadership lessons that extend beyond the realm of fashion.

As the chapter draws to a close, it contemplates the lessons that Zara's story offers to future entrepreneurs, industry leaders, and fashion enthusiasts. The narrative unveils the threads of innovation, resilience, customer-centricity, and sustainability that form the fabric of Zara's success, serving as a source of inspiration for those who aspire to leave their mark on the world.

In the final tapestry of Zara's story, Chapter 10 serves as both a retrospective and a prologue. It encapsulates the brand's enduring legacy while providing insights and lessons that echo into the future—a future where the threads of Zara's influence continue to weave through the ever-changing landscape of fashion.

12

The Unwritten Chapter: Exploring Possibilities and Beyond

Title: "Threads Unexplored: Zara's Future and the Unwritten Chapter"

As we stand at the threshold of Zara's unwritten future, Chapter 11 embarks on an exploration of the possibilities that lie ahead for this fashion titan. It delves into the potential trajectories, innovations, and challenges that might shape the next chapters in Zara's extraordinary narrative.

The chapter begins by considering the evolving nature of consumer preferences and technological advancements. How will Zara continue to integrate cutting-edge technologies, artificial intelligence, and data analytics to enhance the customer experience? The narrative contemplates the intersection of fashion and technology, envisioning possibilities that may redefine the very essence of the retail experience.

Sustainability remains a crucial theme as the chapter unfolds. What new initiatives will Zara undertake to further reduce its environmental impact?

How will the brand contribute to the global movement toward a more sustainable and ethical fashion industry? The narrative explores potential innovations, from eco-friendly materials to circular fashion practices, that could become integral to Zara's future endeavors.

The international landscape beckons Zara to explore uncharted territories. The chapter contemplates the brand's expansion into emerging markets, considering how Zara might adapt its strategies to resonate with diverse cultural nuances while maintaining its global appeal. The narrative envisions Zara's potential role in shaping fashion trends in regions yet untouched by its influence.

Leadership transitions are an inevitable part of any brand's journey. The chapter reflects on how Zara will navigate leadership changes, ensuring a seamless transition that preserves the brand's core values and commitment to innovation. The narrative explores the possibility of new leaders emerging, each contributing a unique chapter to Zara's story.

In the context of an ever-evolving fashion ecosystem, the chapter delves into the concept of conscious consumerism. How will Zara cater to an increasingly aware and socially conscious consumer base? The narrative contemplates the brand's role in influencing consumer behavior and fostering a sense of responsibility in the choices people make.

As the final chapter unfolds, it remains a canvas of possibilities, inviting readers to imagine the next threads that will be woven into Zara's narrative. It's a chapter where uncertainties meet opportunities, and where the brand's ability to innovate, adapt, and inspire will continue to shape its destiny.

Chapter 11 serves as a thought-provoking conclusion, leaving the story of Zara open-ended and inviting readers to envision the brand's future as an unwritten chapter, ready to be woven with the threads of innovation, sustainability, and cultural influence.

13

Threads of Gratitude: Celebrating Zara's Enduring Impact

Title: "Legacy Woven, Gratitude Unveiled: Reflecting on Zara's Enduring Impact"

As we draw the final curtain on the narrative of Zara's incredible journey, Chapter 12 unfolds as a chapter of gratitude and reflection. It is a heartfelt exploration of the brand's enduring impact, the lessons it imparts, and the collective gratitude extended to the people who have contributed to Zara's remarkable story.

The chapter begins by expressing gratitude to the visionary founder, Amancio Ortega. It reflects on his entrepreneurial spirit, leadership legacy, and unwavering commitment to excellence, acknowledging the pivotal role he played in shaping Zara's destiny.

The narrative then extends gratitude to the creative minds behind Zara—the designers, artisans, and innovators who have contributed their talents to the brand's success. It celebrates the collaborative spirit that has allowed Zara to stay at the forefront of fashion, recognizing the dedication and passion of the individuals who breathe life into each collection.

As Zara's story is intrinsically linked with the global fashion landscape, the chapter expresses gratitude to the loyal customer base. It reflects on the symbiotic relationship between Zara and its customers, acknowledging their role in fueling the brand's evolution and making Zara a part of their fashion journey.

The chapter unfolds as a tapestry of appreciation for the broader fashion industry. It recognizes the interconnected web of designers, retailers, artisans, and consumers that collectively shape the dynamic world of fashion. Zara's impact, as outlined throughout the narrative, is woven into this intricate fabric of the fashion ecosystem.

Gratitude is extended to the communities that have been touched by Zara's economic influence. From local artisans to employees in regions across the globe, the narrative acknowledges the positive economic impact Zara has had on various communities.

Finally, the chapter expresses gratitude to the readers and enthusiasts who have joined this narrative journey. It reflects on the shared exploration of Zara's history, impact, and future possibilities, recognizing the collective appreciation for a brand that has left an indelible mark on the global fashion stage.

Chapter 12 serves as a heartfelt conclusion, a moment to pause and express gratitude for the threads of Zara's story. It is an acknowledgment of the brand's lasting impact and an appreciation for the diverse individuals and communities that have contributed to the legacy of one of the fashion industry's most influential players.

14

Summary

"Zara: Threads of Innovation and Legacy" is a comprehensive narrative spanning twelve chapters that unravel the remarkable journey of Zara, from its humble beginnings to its status as a global fashion icon. The story delves into the brand's founding by Amancio Ortega, its pioneering "fast fashion" model, and its transformative impact on the fashion industry.

The chapters explore various facets of Zara's evolution, from technological advancements and sustainability initiatives to its cultural influence and economic legacy. The narrative reflects on Zara's ability to navigate challenges, adapt to changing consumer behaviors, and maintain its position at the forefront of the fashion landscape.

Each chapter unveils threads of innovation, resilience, customer-centricity, and sustainability that form the fabric of Zara's success. The story is woven with insights into the brand's cultural influence, economic contributions, and its ongoing commitment to shaping the future of fashion.

The final chapters invite readers to envision the future of Zara, contemplating possibilities in technology, sustainability, and global expansion. The narrative concludes with gratitude, acknowledging the visionary leadership of Amancio

Ortega, the creative minds behind Zara, its loyal customer base, and the broader fashion industry that collectively contribute to the brand's enduring legacy.

"Zara: Threads of Innovation and Legacy" is a tapestry of inspiration, influence, and anticipation, celebrating a brand that has not only shaped the fashion landscape but also left an indelible mark on global culture and economy.

www.ingramcontent.com/pod-product-compliance
Lightning Source LLC
LaVergne TN
LVHW010444070526
838199LV00066B/6183